INTENTIONAL LIVING

GROUP BIBLE STUDY

WRITTEN BY Jon Nutter

Intentional Living: Group Bible Study
Written by Jon Nutter
© 2020 Warner Press Inc.

Requests for information should be sent to:
Warner Press Inc.
P.O. Box 2499
Anderson, IN 46018
www.warnerpress.org

Kevin Stiffler • Editor
S. Katie Miller • Layout & Design

CONTENTS

The Warner Press *Relevance* Group Bible Studies provide intriguing examinations of topics using the whole of the Scriptures. The guides incorporate various stories and activities to introduce and apply the subject matter, with a Bible study component at the heart of each session. Our goal is to show life-long believers and those new to the faith how to know the Lord intimately while encouraging them to step out and join him in his work with miraculous results.

These flexible studies are ideal for any setting. We know that time is a valuable commodity in today's society, and that's why each book consists of five or six short lessons intended to meet the group's scheduling needs.

L1

Apprenticeship: Following the Way of Jesus

Luke 9:1–6

Main Point

Following Jesus means intentionally apprenticing our lives to learn the way of Jesus.

Background

In the time of Jesus, rabbis (or teachers) had disciples. These followers or apprentices were learners. A disciple adhered to the teacher's instruction and demonstrated the committed way of life of this master. Unlike the cultural practice of the day, Jesus forbade begging for support from house to house. Instead, he prescribed trust in God's provision and a simple lifestyle of self-denial, sacrifice, and service. This meant traveling light; however, it didn't guarantee a life of ease. On the contrary, walking in the way of Jesus requires taking up a cross (originally a Roman device of execution) and dying to oneself.

Gaining Trust through Training

Some years ago, Western educators traded experiential-based training for a knowledge-based teaching model. Unsurprisingly, this educational system has a variety of deficits. Students may know a great deal but do little to employ it. Clearly, knowing a lot about Jesus does not ensure living a lot like Jesus. What is needed for disciples is transformation, not more information.

Effective transformation can come through apprenticeship and a close relational context of observation, experimentation, and practice. Soccer officials learn this way. Referees in training are assigned mentors. Dozens of hours of classroom learning occur and a knowledge test is administered. But most importantly, on-field practice and game experience are gained. Assistant duties are assigned, followed by frequent assessment, extensive coaching, and much encouragement before higher levels of responsibility are granted. Apprenticing engenders trust and confidence in the use of authority.

Have you ever been apprenticed to someone or been assigned a mentor? If so, describe the experience. How you were taught? How did you learn?

How does thinking of the way of Jesus as an apprenticing model of train-ing versus classroom-only teaching change or influence how you relate to Christ, to other followers of Christ, and to would-be followers of Christ?

I. Read Luke 9:1–2.

What are the central tasks Jesus gave his disciples? How or by what means were they to accomplish this work? Why is Luke's summary of Jesus' assignment to the disciples important?

____

____

____

____

Jesus' apprentices were sent to proclaim the kingdom of God. What do you understand this to mean? How is proclaiming God's kingdom the same as or different from sharing Jesus? What are some of the implications of this kingdom assignment?

____

____

____

____

In the contemporary church—especially in the West—there is much suspicion and doubt about those who claim the ability to cast out demons and heal the sick. What is your perspective of and experience with these parts of following Jesus? Have you ever witnessed or participated in either of these miraculous demonstrations? If so, briefly describe the account.

II. Read Luke 9:3–6.

Many view Jesus' words as having a specific and limited initial application to the original disciples, with the broader application to current disciples being not as literal. Others suggest that modern disciples are disobedient or not radical enough in their application. Whatever the application, our understanding of the text is shaped by the cultural context in Jesus' day and contemporary conditions now. Broadly speaking, this passage may be summarized as the imperative to travel light. It promotes a minimalist mindset when it comes the amount of stuff we accumulate and to which we cling. But this isn't strictly limited to physical entanglements. Jesus was demanding that his disciples not let anything hold them back from going. He was requiring that they connect with their community and not waste their time in places where rejected. Have you known anyone who insisted that this passage be taken more literally? Do you think it necessary or helpful to do so? Why or why not?

The expectation of finding hospitality is implicit in Jesus' instructions. What kind of reception were the disciples to be looking for? What would be a parallel in contemporary culture?

Do you think all disciples are called to itinerant ministry? Why or why not? How would you support your position from the Scriptures?

In your opinion, when would it be appropriate to leave a community or relationship in protest?

Obedience to Jesus' direction is observed in the concluding statement of this passage. In some sense this is the purpose of the text, to portray the work of Jesus being accomplished through his apprentices. When and where have you set out on the work of proclamation? Describe how you have been apprenticing in this way.

One Person's Response

A twenty-one-year-old man responded to God's call on his life. He packed all of his belongings into a well-used Honda Accord sedan and made the nearly thousand-mile journey from his Kentucky home to Mid-America Christian University in Oklahoma City. There he would train for ministry, leaving familiar surroundings far behind. Three major moves later, he and his family live far, far away from where he originated. On the final move, it took a caravan of vehicles. Even after selling and giving away significant amounts of their belongings, over ten thousand pounds of stuff was transported. Today, he owns a house filled with furniture, a small plot of ground, and a garage full of automobiles and lawn tools. His ministry has included two decade-long stops on his journey, sometimes serving through conflict and difficulty.

Do you believe this path has been in keeping with what Jesus has in mind for his modern-day followers? Can one still obey Jesus and own a house or have attachments? Why or why not?

What might it mean for you and other followers of Christ to "travel light" on the journey of discipleship?

What Do You Want?

In Luke 9:23–26, Jesus said, "Whoever wants to be my disciple must deny themselves and take up their cross daily and follow me. For whoever wants to save their life will lose it, but whoever loses their life for me will save it. What good is it for someone to gain the whole world, and yet lose or forfeit their very self? Whoever is ashamed of me and my words, the Son of Man will be ashamed of them when he comes in his glory and in the glory of the Father and of the holy angels." Personal desires and self-denial are explicit in Jesus' description of what it means to be his disciple.

How would you interpret what Jesus said we must want and what it is we must be willing to deny? Give specific examples you think may apply.

Jesus contrasted saving versus losing and gaining versus forfeiting. What is at risk for those who choose self or gaining stuff over Jesus? Describe a time when you experienced this truth of losing and gaining.

____

____

____

____

____

____

What is the incentive to avoid being ashamed of Jesus? How do you guard against shame and fear?

____

____

____

____

____

One-Way Journey

Over 150 years ago, some courageous souls became known as "one-way missionaries." Instead of steamer trunks, they packed their belongings in caskets and purchased one-way tickets to fields of endeavor from which they knew they would never return. Methodist James Calvert (1813–1892) was committed to reaching the indigenous peoples of the Fiji Islands. The captain of his ship warned, "You will lose your life and the lives of those with you if you go among such savages."

Calvert replied, "We died before we came here."

In the twentieth century, Jim Elliot and his companions gave their lives in Ecuador. Elliot famously journaled, "He is no fool who gives what he cannot keep to gain that which he cannot lose."

Reflect on the willingness of these people to sacrifice self, family connections, and possessions in order to be an apprentice of Jesus. What can you do to be better prepared and to function more fully as a follower of the way of Jesus?

Closing Prayer

Master Jesus, we thank you for your example of what it means to live intentionally for God's kingdom. Thank you for the invitation to apprentice. We acknowledge our difficulty in trusting you, denying ourselves, living sacrificially, and speaking up on your behalf. Forgive us. We profess our willingness to be instructed and trained. Help us as we seek unashamedly to live according to your design, to act in your authority, and to serve with your power. Amen.■

Acting Wisely, not Anxiously

Matthew 6:19–34; 7:21–29

Main Point

Acting wisely by building on a foundation of trust frees us from anxiety and the pressure to accumulate treasure on earth.

Background

Embedded in the second half of perhaps Jesus' most famous sermon, these passages offer us kingdom perspectives and practices. Here we find warnings against sins common in every society but especially so in our Western consumeristic and individualistic context. Jesus offered warnings against being greedy, materialistic, or anxious about securing our own well-being apart from God's provision and care. Jesus located the source of these sins in in our hearts, where misplaced priorities and misaligned perspectives reflect a lack of trust or fidelity. Those who worry live with fear and insecurity rather than with confidence moored in a stable foundation.

Building on the Right Foundation

Thunderstorms, tornadoes, flash floods, grassfires, and theft are part and parcel of life in the Midwestern United States. People learn to adapt by planting trees for wind breaks, choosing high ground, raising their foundations, building storm cellars, and employing personal security systems. Yet even with the advances in construction techniques, flood control, fire suppression, weather forecasting, and security, people still lose everything when a major storm, flood, or fire races through a community. Living through a big storm can be overwhelming. Experiencing flooding of one's home, being the victim of a home invasion, or watching helplessly as others lose their property and possessions to fire is devastating. As the years pass, learning how little security there is in the accumulation of goods is imperative. Nothing is more essential or valuable than building a life of trusting Jesus.

Have you or someone you've known experienced the loss of things due to flood, storm, fire, theft, etc.? If so, describe how you or this person felt and responded. What sort of self-learning took place through the experience?

Over time, how has experience tempered or shaped your approach to accumulation and possessions? Do you worry more or less now about your stuff? Explain.

I. Read Matthew 6:19–24.

Jesus' sayings contain multiple contrasts between common practice and his prescription for his followers. Identify these contrasts. Which of them resonates most powerfully in your life? Why?

Growing in trust often means having our commitments put to the test of stress. How has your loyalty and service to God been tested by financial pressures or the desire for security in wealth? Describe a season or incident. What helped you trust God?

II. Read Matthew 6:25–32.

According to Jesus, worrying about the things you need is a pagan practice. Trusting in God's character and provision is his prescription for his followers. In which way do you most often live, and why?

What do you find yourself worrying about most often? Why? What was your most recent worry?

In the past, how has God demonstrated his trustworthiness? What incident most recently demonstrated God's faithfulness to you?

III. Read Matthew 6:33–34.

Describe in practical terms what you think it means to seek first God's kingdom. Has there ever been a time or circumstance when you felt as if you were following this counsel yet still found yourself lacking something essential? How did you respond? How did you reconcile your experience with today's text? How did the circumstance end up being resolved?

____

____

____

____

____

Could putting money in savings or planning ahead be considered "worrying about tomorrow"? Why or why not? How might Jesus' words here be misapplied as an excuse for someone to be lazy or careless? Describe a time when someone made such a misapplication. How do we find the proper application of this concept?

____

____

____

____

____

IV. Read Matthew 7:21–29.

We live in a time where many claim the name of Christ and seem to be engaged in the work of the Kingdom. What is your reaction to Jesus' declaration that he will reject many who make such statements? On what basis did Jesus seem to indicate this rejection comes? How is it even possible to prophesy, cast out demons, and perform miracles in Jesus' name but still be rejected by him? Aren't these things examples of doing the Father's will? Explain.

Jesus closed his sermon with a parable. This short story contains a central point cloaked in the portrayal of two kinds of persons, the wise and the foolish. Their circumstances don't differ, only their choice as to whether to practice Jesus' teaching. How do you go about evaluating your own practice of Jesus' teaching? Do you find more comfort (security) or conviction (insecurity) in Jesus' conclusion? Explain.

A Covenant of Stewardship

Inspired by the faith of evangelist George Mueller, Mr. Mallipudi committed his life to providing for orphans in his home country of India. Mallipudi immigrated to southern California in 1981 with his wife and three boys, and soon added a daughter. Even in unsettled economic times, Mallipudi saw unprecedented opportunity for one willing to work hard. Covenanting to fully trust and rely upon God, Mallipudi set out to faithfully return tithes and offerings to the Lord. Each year for decades he increased his giving by at least one percent. Today, he continues living in southern California on less than fifty percent of his income. He ministers frequently in India, often for a month or more at a time, supports numerous missionaries there, and makes frequent and significant financial gifts both domestically and abroad from funds he has accumulated. Mallipudi credits God's trustworthiness for all the blessings he has received and any impact his own efforts have made.

What is your reaction to Mr. Mallipudi's story? Who has inspired your approach to trusting God with your finances, and how?

____

____

____

What would be a good place for you to start as a covenant with God to trust him for provision?

____

____

____

Wise and Foolish Builders

At church, many children still learn the song about the wise man and the foolish man based on the parable Jesus told in Matthew 7:24–27. Older people sometimes lament, "If I could just go back in time knowing what I know now!" What a shame if it takes us until old age to gain life-changing wisdom, when we have limited time and opportunities to apply it. The rains come down, the streams rise, and the winds beat against everyone's house. The goal is not to avoid these storms but for the house to still be standing when the storms have passed.

Based on Jesus' teaching from today's study, what is required to be wise? Why do you say so? What does this look like in practical terms?

What is the temptation to build one's house on sand instead of on the rock? Why would anyone be foolish enough to do this?

Last Words and Witness

John Wesley was an Anglican priest, enthusiastic evangelist, social reformer, and the reluctant founder of Methodism. His Aldersgate experience radically altered the tenor and course of his life, his ministry, and the church around the world. Often reviled by skeptics, he died in the company of friends on March 2, 1791. His last words: "The best of all is, God is with us." Wesley died nearly penniless—but rich.

Most of us will have very little say on how or when the end comes. Perhaps some will see it through a long tunnel and have long and painful goodbyes. For others it will come with blinding speed. Perhaps Wesley long thought about his last utterance, or perhaps it came with the prompting of the Spirit in that moment. Whatever the case, his words have been both inspiring and a comfort to many. More inspiring still: his example of faithful giving and charity.

Spend a few moments considering your last testimony or legacy as a child of God. What would you like to say to those who see you pass or who will remember your passing?

____

____

____

What would you like those closest to you to say about you at your funeral?

____

____

____

Closing Prayer

Father God, thank you for the assurance of your provision. We ask you to remind us of your ability to take care of our every need as we observe your care for the people and creatures we encounter on a daily basis. Calm our anxious thoughts with the comfort of your presence. Give us clarity about our Kingdom contributions. Guard our eyes and hearts. Show us how to trust you fully as we give ourselves away freely. Amen. ∎

L3

Aligning Habits

1 Timothy 4:1–9

Main Point

Following Jesus requires caring for our bodies as part of fully training ourselves to honor Christ in our witness to others.

Background

Paul wrote two letters to offer encouragement and further equip his protégé Timothy. In the first he confronted philosophical errors and practical misapplications of the gospel. Among these were a developing Gnosticism (which viewed the material or flesh as evil), a misguided ascetism, and influential but controversial Jewish practices. Each error in its own way pressured early Christians to conform themselves in a manner contradictory to the message of the gospel of Christ. Paul sought to both remind and inform his readers of how they might nourish their lives—body and soul—by aligning their habits of mind and body with the life and truth of Jesus.

Neglecting the Body, Getting Sick Spiritually

For most of my twenties I enthusiastically engaged in challenging ministry contexts. My priority was spiritual pursuits or ministry activity. But during this time an athletic, active, and otherwise fit young adult slowly and almost imperceptibly became a sedentary, unhealthy, lethargic thirty-year old. The resulting physical and spiritual crisis changed the way I approached life and ministry.

It seems that we easily fall prey to habits of physical neglect and poor nutrition and even become guilty of abusing our own bodies, either actively or passively. Have we have accepted a false dilemma not inherent in our faith? Do we believe our physical health is less important than our spiritual health (as if they are not related at all)? Wise counsel from a medical doctor, a clear sense of God's direction, and encouragement from others led to the incorporation of physical disciplines in my spiritual habits.

How important do you view taking care of your physical body as a part of your spiritual walk and witness? Have you always felt this way? Why or why not?

____

____

____

____

____

What counsel might you offer to someone in your life who is consistently
neglecting his or her health or physical well-being while making spiritual-
sounding excuses?

I. Read 1 Timothy 4:1–2.

Being taught and led by the Holy Spirit should be a high value for Jesus followers. Paul allowed that even those who start out with the best of intentions can be led astray or abandon the faith. From where or whom do teachings that lead people astray and are contrary to the gospel come?

____

____

____

____

What feelings do the possibility of personally abandoning the faith and the presence of deceivers, demons, and liars among Christian teachers stir in you? How have you dealt with times of discouragement when you were tempted to give up or when a high-profile or respected leader let you down?

____

____

____

____

What does it mean to have a "seared conscience" (v 2)? Without naming names, list some examples of situations where people claim the name of Christ but speak or act in ways that show no concern for the care of others.

____

____

____

II. Read 1 Timothy 4:3–6.

Asceticism and Gnosticism were two of the teachings infecting early Christian groups. These Greek philosophies prescribed harsh treatment of the body or flesh and abstinence from physical pleasures, rejecting the inherent goodness of God's creation and suggesting strategies for avoiding being corrupted by it. In addition, the highest spiritual attainment was limited to the few and required special knowledge. Only through strict avoidance of the corruption of the flesh could this knowledge be secured. How did Paul counter these philosophies? What prescriptions or practices did he encourage?

In what ways have people taken the good things God has created and twisted their use for harmful or self-serving purposes?

What assurances and encouragements did Paul offer for adhering to his counsel?

____

____

____

III. Read 1 Timothy 4:7–9.

Godliness was of ultimate concern for Paul, but here he noted that physical training was of some value and that his teaching deserved full acceptance. This physical training wasn't the harsh asceticism of the false teachers and their prescribed abstinence from all things pleasurable. What, if any, spiritual benefits have you seen from taking care of your body? How has neglect of your physical body impacted your spiritual practice?

____

____

____

____

In what ways do myths or superstitions impact the beliefs and behavior of well-intentioned believers?

____

____

____

What might be some appropriate ways to incorporate physical training in your daily routine? What factors might make this difficult to do? How can you combat these obstacles?

____

____

____

____

____

Why does the concept of the rewards of our faith often seem to be focused on "the life to come" (i.e., heaven) rather than on the "present life" (v 8)?

____

____

____

____

____

Effective Training

Cross-training is the practice of employing multiple disciplines or activities to functionally train all major muscle groups. CrossFit is a popular expression of this approach. It adapts and adopts physical exercises used to train military personnel for service in harsh conditions. The combination of cardio-building and strength-enhancing movements, with a variety of options and sequences, makes it incredibly popular and effective. Almost anyone can start where they are and begin to see instant progress. By focusing on a full-body workout and functional strength, cross-trainers avoid common overuse injuries, lose weight, and gain flexibility, endurance, and strength.

The analogy to spirituality is obvious. Body, mind, and soul are integral to our spiritual training in godliness. It would be ridiculous to neglect traditional spiritual disciplines of prayer, Bible reading, worship, and the like and think we could become godly. Yet we often neglect physical exercise or intellectual development and think we can grow functionally stronger or avoid spiritual injury. Neglecting body or mind imperils our spiritual health in ways similar to neglecting other spiritual disciplines does.

How have you effectively trained your body, mind, and soul? How has your approach changed as your physical, mental, or spiritual seasons have changed?

Self-Care

Paul wrote in Romans 12:1–2, "Therefore, I urge you, brothers and sisters, in view of God's mercy, to offer your bodies as a living sacrifice, holy and pleasing to God—this is your true and proper worship. Do not conform to the pattern of this world, but be transformed by the renewing of your mind. Then you will be able to test and approve what God's will is—his good, pleasing and perfect will." As you read and reflect on these words, consider God's great mercy. Many of us can think of moments when our health, well-being, or lives were imperiled.

Describe a health scare, accident, or near-death experience that reminded you of the importance of taking care of your body.

____

____

____

____

Is there any part of your body or your physical make-up you are withholding, misusing, or ashamed of? What might be holding you back from offering this part of yourself to God? How would renewing your thinking about your body impact the way you align your habits?

____

____

____

Total Alignment

Since 2001 she has completed two full Ironman Triathlons and nineteen marathons. During her first race, she hit the wall at mile seventeen. She credits scripture memory for giving her the inspiration to finish. Knowing the power of the Word of God to inspire, she started a business to help people share their faith through fitness. Her products inspire thousands to care for their bodies and to renew their minds with the Scriptures. Doing difficult endurance races for more than twenty years makes her walk with Christ look attractive to others seeking a fulfilling life.

Our witness can't be quantified by the number of steps we walk, the minutes we exercise, or the miles we run or ride. It is defined by the consistency with which we take care of our bodies and continue to align our habits of thought and action with Christ.

Consistency requires starting lines, mile markers, finish lines, and training plans. What do each of these look like in your own attempt at aligning your physical and spiritual habits?

If you had two decades to train physically and spiritually, what would you prefer your accomplishments to look like?

____

____

____

____

____

____

Closing Prayer

Creator God who made us and knows our frame, we offer ourselves to you—body, mind, and spirit. Help us to remember in whose image we are made. Make us mindful of the honor and care our temples of your Spirit deserve. Strengthen our commitment to consistently training for the marathon of a life of witness. Give us the courage to take first steps physically and to overcome spiritual obstacles. May we not conform but be transformed. Amen. ∎

Avoiding Immorality and Idolatry

1 Corinthians 6:12–20

Main Point

Avoiding immorality and idolatry is a sacrifice of worship and a powerful witness to the world of our trust in Christ; self-denial must be Spirit-enabled to have value for transformation.

Background

Paul often penned letters in response to concerns, questions, or problems in particular locales such as Corinth and Colossae. While some of our understanding is conjecture, context and historical analysis give us sufficient insight to suggest that these letters address similar issues. The Greco-Roman world was cosmopolitan, prosperous, philosophically curious, fragmented or partisan, spiritually pluralistic, and corrupt morally. Believing in Christ's life, death, and resurrection suggested specific practical applications which, within this culture, required the rejection of certain common practices, perspectives, and philosophies. The avoidance of idolatry and sexual immorality were chief among these. Then and now, Christianity stands in contradiction to common philosophies and practices.

Philosophy and Theology

We might define *philosophy* as the study of the contemplation of what is right and wrong. Philosophy explores the nature of morality, and it considers how people should live their lives in relation to others. We might define *theology* as those things that are taught *by* God, those things that are taught *about* God, and those things that lead *to* God.

Philosophy or theology—which have you spent more time studying? When did you undertake this study? What prompted your study?

____

____

____

____

____

Do you have a favorite philosopher or theologian? If so, who? What significant contributions has this person made to your understanding of how the world works and your place in it?

____

____

____

____

____

Philosophers and theologians can offer differing answers to life's biggest questions. One of these divergences is in the area of morality versus immorality. How do you believe you acquired your sense of morality? When did you receive it?

How has your understanding of life, philosophy, and theology changed over the years?

I. **Read** 1 Corinthians 6:12–13.

In what ways have you seen alcohol, food, sex, possessions, or other things "master" well-intentioned believers who claim that their use of or focus on these things is their personal "right"?

____

____

____

____

Paul contradicted common wisdom or slogans of the philosophers of his day with his own theological clarification of the relationship between what we say or do, eat or serve and how we treat our bodies. Here he delineated between what our rights are versus what is beneficial, between our personal desires and God's intentions. What seems to be Paul's main point in the concluding statement of verse 13? Why is this important or relevant to us?

____

____

____

____

What do you think it means that God will destroy both our stomachs and the food we eat (v 13)?

____

____

II. Read 1 Corinthians 6:14–17.

Paul invoked the resurrection and body-of-Christ imagery, as well as Judeo-Christian teaching regarding marriage, and concluded by introducing "spirit" (v 17). Paul was clearly combatting a dualistic understanding of human nature which suggested that the material/flesh is inherently evil or worthless. How does the idea that your body was made for the Lord affect you emotionally?

Union with Christ is not literal as we might define the term and it is not sexual, yet it *is* physical in addition to being spiritual. What are some of the broad implications of this with respect to our moral behavior and the care of our bodies?

How does verse 16 explain the emotional and spiritual troubles that come from having multiple sexual contacts throughout one's life rather than having one's spouse as the only sexual partner?

How does the intimacy of a physical sexual union help us to better understand the unity we can experience with the Lord in our spirits, as we are filled with his Spirit?

III. Read 1 Corinthians 6:18–20.

On what basis did Paul counsel us to flee from sexual immorality? In what ways can we flee as Paul recommended here?

Honoring God with our bodies is not just a prohibition against immorality; it is a prescription for worship. Is the fact that God, through his Spirit, dwells in us a "heavy" piece of knowledge that restricts us, or does it bring power, life, and freedom? Explain.

At what price were we bought? In what ways can we remind ourselves and others of this on a regular basis?

What are some positive ways we might treat our bodies in an effort to honor God?

Confinement or Cooperation?

In Colossians 2 and 3, Paul warned against being taken captive by philosophy, human tradition, and spiritual forces. He contrasted the value of these things with that of Christ. Two thousand years later, the battle still rages.

Why do you think it is so easy for so many people to fall prey to false asceticism or legalistic rituals? Are *you* more likely to mindlessly follow rules or be a bit of a rebel? Why? What benefit, if any, have you found in rituals and regulations?

How is being captured or submitting to rules different from choosing to cooperate with the Holy Spirit through disciplines? Do you think Paul discounted all rituals and traditions, or might there be some value in willingly forsaking certain things and observing others? Explain.

What have you found most helpful in restraining your own self-indulgent habits? In simple terms, what philosophy or theology have you adopted to give you guidance for how you live?

Direction and Focus

As believers who choose to worship Christ, there are certain choices we make regarding the way we live. Our ability to avoid immorality is a choice empowered by the resurrection. Care must be taken to prioritize our pursuits—the positive alternative to simple avoidance. Both our heart (emotions) and mind (thinking) must be directed. Unless we intend to isolate ourselves from all outside contact and influence, this is a much more effective way to live. Effort is required, but the results lead to the life, freedom, and renewal in Christ that Paul wrote about.

Paul said in Colossians 3:1–2 that we should focus "on things above." What are these things? What are some tools to redirect our focus when it has wandered?

Apart from asceticism and legalism, what does it look like to put to death immorality and avoid idolatry as Paul urged in Colossians 3:5? Why do you think he used such dramatic terms to describe our attitude toward these things?

Spiritual Motivation

Modern asceticism—severe self-discipline and avoidance of all forms of indulgence—might include vegetarians, monastics, those practicing celibacy, or those choosing to abstain from consuming alcoholic beverages. It might also include those who rigorously train their bodies for athletic contests and deny themselves desserts or fatty foods. Simple fasting could be considered a form of asceticism.

Historical asceticism made these choices a moral imperative. Self-denial was compulsory in order to attain a higher spiritual plane. However, for authentic followers of Christ the value of self-denial isn't in what we achieve through our own willfulness. The value of self-denial is found in the freedom from being constrained to indulge or enslaved by our natural desires. In this liberty we find the ability to focus on Christ more fully. Our motivation isn't the avoidance of immorality or idolatry as much as it is the pursuit of purity and appropriate worship of Jesus.

How have your own choices about what you eat or drink or you own sexuality been morally or spiritually motivated?

Has your experience of self-denial been more freeing or burdensome? In
what ways?

____

____

____

____

How can you choose to bring greater focus on and clarity to Christ through
self-denial?

____

____

____

____

Closing Prayer

Lord, we confess the temptation of the traps of legalism, asceticism, immorality, and idolatry. We have often valued our own efforts over the endowment of the Holy Spirit. Give us confidence in Christ and the power of the resurrection. We long to conform to his image. We desire holiness in our hearts that is expressed through our hands. May our worship please you as we focus on things above, and may we put to death our sinful desires. Amen.∎

L 5

Acknowledging Lordship

Proverbs 3:5–6, 9–10, 13–18; Colossians 3:15–17

Main Point

Acknowledging Christ's Lordship is the wise path to prosperity and long life.

Background

Proverbs is a collection of godly wisdom and instructions commonly attributed to Solomon. The Proverbs are presented as preparation for life and leadership from a royal father to his son, most often in small groupings of related verses. Pithy statements, often in parallel, employ repetition and other poetic devices to strengthen their effect and make them memorable. Much of Proverbs is not religious in the strictest sense, but the whole book reflects a worldview that looks to the Creator for guidance in all of life. Meditating upon the Proverbs proves their worth. Godly wisdom—including acknowledging Jesus Christ as Lord—should be taught within the family of God.

What Is Wisdom Worth?

What good is wisdom anyway? Is there anything to gain from increasing in knowledge and understanding? How do I become wise? Do I need a college education or more? Isn't experience the best teacher, and if it is, do I have to experience all of the negative lessons myself or can I learn from others' experience? These are serious questions that deserve our consideration. In the biblical tradition, Solomon is considered the wisest person or teacher (save Jesus) who ever lived. In today's society, people are pragmatic, practical, and looking for approaches that pay off. Proverbs offers us a path to long life and prosperity if we're willing to acknowledge God as our Lord.

Who is the wisest person you know? What is it about this individual that makes him or her wise?

How have you learned wisdom the hard way in the past? What's the most expensive lesson you ever learned?

Why is acknowledging someone else as an authority or as wise, especially with respect to something we thought differently about, so difficult for many of us?

I. **Read** Proverbs 3:5–6.

"Trust and obey, for there's no other way to be happy in Jesus," says the old hymn. How much trust and obedience does the writer of Proverbs say is imperative? Why?

____

____

____

____

Partial obedience is disobedience. How has leaning on your own understanding gotten you off course in life?

____

____

____

The word rendered as *acknowledge* in this passage (NIV) used to be translated as "submit." What are the similarities and differences between these terms? Why is the idea that acknowledgment means more than hearing or seeing important in this context?

____

____

____

____

What outcome is the consequence of heeding the wisdom here? How has this played out in your own experience?

____

____

____

____

II. Read Proverbs 3:9–10.

Honoring the Lord is an important parallel to acknowledging or submitting to the Lord. The concept of "firstfruits" was imbedded in the law of the Hebrews and placed in parallel to the concept of honor. What might it mean or look like to honor the Lord with the firstfruits—the first and best portion of your wealth or income?

____

____

____

These verses seem to indicate that things will not just go well, they will go *very* well when we practice godly financial stewardship. Why do you think so many people struggle to heed godly wisdom when it comes to wealth management and stewardship?

____

____

____

III. Read Proverbs 3:13–18.

"Finding" and "gaining" in these verses describes not an accidental pursuit but an intentional effort that brings blessing. Wisdom's worth is compared to items that are mined and considered valuable, in part, because of their difficulty in acquiring. How does the idea that wisdom must be "mined" strike you? How much effort have you recently been putting into gaining understanding? Explain.

How has the acquisition of wisdom and understanding proven valuable to you—including relationally and spiritually?

IV. Read Colossians 3:15–17.

In the New Testament, Christ is the wisdom of God (1 Cor 1:24). As Paul offered this ethical "holiness code" in Colossians, he exhorted his readers regarding the peace of Christ and the message of Christ. What role is the peace of Christ to have in our hearts? Where and how is the message of Christ to dwell? Explain.

Acknowledging God in all our ways includes receiving teaching and admonishment from other wise believers. In what medium did Paul encourage this to be communicated? Is this surprising to you? Why or why not? What impact should this have on our corporate gatherings, song selections, and ways of singing?

In the name of Jesus we acknowledge God in word and deed. What is the attitude prescribed behind this acknowledgment? Why do you think this is so important to the process? How has being thankful made it easier for you to acknowledge God?

The Meaning of Discipleship

The late Dallas Willard wrote and lectured extensively about spiritual disciplines and spiritual formation. He once said, "Discipleship means learning to acknowledge God in all we do—and it takes a lot of learning. You actually never get done learning because you are always learning, and increasingly you are able to acknowledge him in all of your ways. You are able to do everything you do in word or deed on behalf of the Lord Jesus Christ" (see http://www.dwillard.org/articles/individual/knowing-how-to-acknowledge-god). Willard was describing the long and arduous process of growing in our acknowledgment of the Lordship of Christ. He maintained that progress is possible and observable, even to the extent of fully doing God's will (at least in moments and seasons).

How do you react to Willard's assertion? How long have you been learning? How close are you to meeting the standard he described? Explain.

____

____

____

____

Describe your experience of growing in the ability to acknowledge God's ways or doing all things for his glory.

____

____

____

Describe a time or situation in which God's wisdom took precedence over your own understanding as you consciously chose to submit to what you knew was God's will.

Acknowledging God

Around the world, there are millions of Christians who live in places where they experience high levels of persecution just for following Jesus. Acknowledging allegiance to Jesus in these places is literally life-threatening. Despite growing hostility in some contexts, few Western believers are at risk of shedding blood or imprisonment for their witness.

Jesus declared in Matthew 10:32–33, "Whoever acknowledges me before others, I will also acknowledge before my Father in heaven. But whoever disowns me before others, I will disown before my Father in heaven." Make a list of the people in your life before whom you need to acknowledge God. Thinking categorically can give you a more expansive list. Think through your family, work, friendship, acquaintance, church, customer, vendor, and social contact lists.

What might it look like for you to acknowledge God before these people? What tangible actions of acknowledgement could you take in the coming week?

Intentional Acknowledgement

A wise and respected mentor offered a sixteen-year-old a simple Bible study plan and perhaps the best advice he could when he said, "Read one chapter of Proverbs each day of the month. Intentionally memorize and meditate on at least one verse a day." Soon afterward this young man became conflicted and confused about his life's direction. Contradictory advice and temptations on multiple fronts assaulted him. But Proverbs 3 became his signature scripture. Trust, stewardship, and the pursuit of wisdom took precedence in his life. He hasn't always been faithful to the reading plan over the years, but the wisdom it provided has proven more valuable than any other counsel he has ever received.

Read or recite Proverbs 3:5–6, 9–10 aloud with the other members of your group. If you don't already know these verses by heart, commit to memorizing them in the week ahead. Below, describe how these verses have impacted your intentional living.

In what area(s) of life (relationships, finances, work, choices, etc.) might you need to be more intentional in acknowledging God? Explain.

Closing Prayer

God of wisdom, Lord of life, we acknowledge your Lordship over all the earth and every facet of our lives. You who know better than us what we need, we ask you to meet us in this moment and grant us peace. May we know what it means to trust your ways over and above our own. Give us the courage and grace to acknowledge you publicly with gratitude and praise. May our lives reflect your wisdom. Amen. ∎

Acquiring Character and Accepting Our Calling

Ephesians 2:8–10; 4:1–3; 2 Peter 1:1–10

Main Point

Our character and calling must be pursued with perseverance and empowered by grace in order to be accomplished.

Background

The apostles Peter and Paul had unique calls but similar counsel with respect to character formation and fulfilling God's call. Each was concerned that Christ-followers stand firm in grace and advance forcefully in the power of the Holy Spirit. Paul, in his correspondence with the Ephesian church, laid the foundation of God's intention and described in detail the identity God gives. He then moved to the imperatives of one's calling. Peter similarly reminded his readers of their identity and what they have received before urging their diligent pursuit of their call. Our own mission or calling is too important to be lazy or half-hearted in its pursuit.

Beyond Good Intentions

"The road to hell is paved with good intentions." This well-known saying suggests that the good we intend to do doesn't always get accomplished, that our impact isn't always what we intend it to be. Predicting the outcomes of our efforts can be difficult. The good we intend often has unforeseen consequences. But for significant and positive results to occur, our intentions must be converted to actions.

Intentionally pursuing character and calling requires our most persistent efforts. Grace, while it cannot be earned, isn't opposed to effort. Our submitted efforts, combined with God's purpose and power, will produce his desired outcomes both in us and through us.

In what area of your life (health, family, work, faith, etc.) do you have the most difficulty converting intentions into positive actions? Explain. What excuses or explanations do you commonly employ? What is it you need to do to move from good intentions to positive actions?

Describe a time or scenario when what you intended with your efforts didn't turn out the way you had hoped. How did it feel to see your good intentions thwarted or fail? Has failure changed your approach to similar situations? If so, how?

I. Read Ephesians 2:8–10.

In this passage, Paul described the identity of all Christians, God's intention for them, and how God brings it about. What did Paul say is true about the Ephesians and, by extension, us? What does this mean?

____

____

____

____

____

The term _handiwork_ (NIV) can also be rendered as "masterpiece." This indicates that we are individually shaped or formed by God's personal involvement. Each of us is unique, "fearfully and wonderfully made" (Ps 139:14). How does it make you feel when you think about God designing you so intricately and intentionally? Explain.

____

____

____

____

What things about you do you believe indicate your uniqueness? What works do you feel called to do? How has God affirmed these traits and tasks?

____

____

____

____

____

II. Read Ephesians 4:1–3.

We are each, as individuals, called to action—but not in isolation. Relationship is a huge component of all of our callings. Our personal mission can't be accomplished apart from others. Examine the traits listed and the approach and effort Paul demanded. With which of these do you struggle the most? Explain.

____

____

____

____

____

We often give ourselves more credit for the level of effort we're exerting than the level of effort others are giving. When it comes to relationships, it can be easy to say or assume others aren't giving equal effort. Think of a relationship that is difficult. How do you assess the effort the other person is giving?

____

____

____

____

On a scale of 1 to 5, with 1 being "hardly at all" and 5 being "to a great extent," how hard are you trying to "keep the unity of the Spirit"? What are the indicators of your effort?

____

____

____

____

III. Read 2 Peter 1:1–10.

Understanding what we possess and our position in relationship to God is crucial to having the motivation to pursue our callings. What did Peter describe as ours to claim and possess?

____

____

____

What is the prerequisite of grace and peace from God? How is this acquired?

Participating in the divine nature doesn't make us divine ourselves, but it does result in us escaping the corruption caused by evil desires. What does this suggest to you about what it means to have an authentic faith?

Peter prescribed making every effort to add to our faith specific attributes that express themselves in community. What is the promised outcome of this diligence? Why is this important?

The same prescription is applied to confirming our callings and elections. Why is this diligence important? How has being less than diligent impacted your walk with Christ? In what way(s) are you prone to stumble?

The Importance of Love

In training camp during 1961, the summer after a heart-breaking loss to the Philadelphia Eagles in the NFC championship, the venerable Green Bay Packers coach Vince Lombardi famously held up the oblong-shaped pigskin in front of his team and said, "Gentlemen, this is a football." He then methodically and carefully covered the fundamentals of the game. Coaching week after week by pointing to the little yet most important things, Lombardi demanded the best effort from his players. Their efforts culminated in the 37-to-0 defeat of the New York Giants in the league-wide championship.

Diligent, persistent pursuit of mastering the basics of Christian faith and practice doesn't win championships, but it does produce something greater: spiritual fruit. Those who wish to be effective followers of Christ should huddle around the playbook Peter offered and pay careful attention to the attributes and actions in which he coached his readers.

Nothing is more fundamental to the Christian faith than love. Describe and define what love is and looks like.

What are some practical ways you could deepen your love for the others in
your group and for those outside the group?

____

____

____

____

____

____

Explain how you would define each of the following terms. Is each more attitude or action or a bit of both? Why?

goodness ____

____

knowledge ____

____

self-control ____

____

perseverance ____

____

godliness ____

____

mutual affection ____

____

love ____

____

On a scale of 1 to 5, with 1 being "hardly at all" and 5 being "to a great extent," what kind of effort are you making to add these things to your faith? Why do you say so?

____

____

____

____

____

Pick one of these attributes and describe what it would look like practically in your life to make the effort to add it to your faith.

____

____

____

____

Staying Effective

Peter described the possibility of falling prey to three negative spiritual conditions. Believers can be nearsighted, blind, or forget what Christ has accomplished on their behalf. A believer's being spiritually blind is seemingly an oxymoron, and yet a lack of vision or spiritual perception occurs and is observed when people act in ways obviously incompatible with their faith. Others are nearsighted or suffering from spiritual myopia; they have difficulty with clarity or focus on things beyond a limited distance. The third condition is spiritual amnesia. Forgetfulness is frequently warned against within God's Word. Believers are often reminded to remember, an act of willful focus on what has occurred in the past. Like the physical condition, spiritual amnesia or other forms of forgetfulness may be triggered by trauma or illness.

What might contribute to or be the cause of a believer's spiritual blindness? What did Peter encourage to assist us in the avoidance of this condition?

What is the outcome of being spiritually nearsighted? Why is this dangerous? How might this condition be addressed or corrected?

____

____

____

____

____

What are some of the causes of spiritual amnesia or forgetfulness? How do we go about cultivating spiritual memory?

____

____

____

____

Closing Prayer

Gracious Father, thank you for the privilege of being your children. We are honored by the invitation to serve at your good pleasure. We are amazed by your intention to shape us into masterpieces, useful vessels for accomplishing good works. We are awed at the knowledge that you have given us everything we need to live as you intended. We commit ourselves to the effort you have asked of us. Strengthen our resolve as we seek to honor you. Amen. ∎

Notes